Coping Through a Crisis:

32+ DAILY MEDITATIONS, POWER-FUL DECLARATIONS AND POSITIVE AFFIRMATIONS THAT WILL HELP YOU MANAGE TOUGH TIMES

Vestina Oates ~ Dr. Empowerment

Coping Through a Crisis: 32+ Daily Meditations, Powerful Declarations and Positive Affirmations That Will Help You Manage Tough Times

Send email of this request to vestinao@hotmail.com

Unless otherwise noted, all scripture references taken from the Holy Bible, New International Version® (NIV) 2011 by Biblica Inc. ™.
All rights reserved.

The advice and strategies contained herein may not be suitable for every situation. This work is sold with the understanding that the author is not engaged in rendering medical, legal, or other professional advice or services. If professional assistance is required, the services of a competent professional person should be sought. The author shall not be liable for damages arising herefrom. The fact that an individual, organization, or website is referred to in this work as a citation and/or potential source of further information does not mean that the author endorses the information the individual, organization, or website may provide or recommendations they/it may make.

Edited by: Vashtina Brown (Lead) (vashtina@gmail.com) & Leslene Anderson (Support)

Formatted by: Jahzema Gabrielle (jahzemagabrielle@gmail.com)

Self-published. Kingston, Jamaica.

Dedication

This book is dedicated to my sons Mikhail Morris and Terrence Carter as well as to the Tribe. The Tribe is an interdenominational group headed by Apostle Dr. Patience Oti who meets virtually every day to pray and study the Bible in its entirety.

CONTENTS

Introduction

INTRODUCTION

We all face crises at different moments of our lives, but our ability to navigate through these challenges successfully, is what makes or breaks us. This book proffers practical advice on how to transform your heart, mind and soul by changing your negative thought patterns into positive ones to rise above adversities. Through the use of these daily meditations, powerful declarations and positive affirmations, you will experience breakthroughs and life-changing moments in the days ahead. Each day is completed with three powerful declarations or affirmations because the number three represents completeness and fulfilment. It also represents divine wholeness an perfection. This book is backed by scientific research and employs a holistic approach; it is guaranteed to produce remarkable changes in your life. So, get ready to transform your pain into purpose, trauma into triumph and loss into gain. You will be able to influence your subconscious mind to access new beliefs. Ultimately, you are teaching your brain a new way of thinking about yourself and the world around you. May the meditations, declarations and affirmations in this book change the trajectory of your life emotionally, mentally, financially, physically and spiritually.

HOW TO READ THIS BOOK

As you begin reading your daily meditations, declarations and affirmations, open your heart, mind and spirit. Read this book every day and allow it to journey with you on your path to success. It is the connection with the words that will truly awaken your spirit and take you where you want to go. You will need a pen or pencil and a book or loose paper. After reading each declaration/affirmation, affix your thumbprint / signature to seal and establish it. In doing so, you are solidifying these thoughts in your subconscious. Get ready for an overflow of goodness, prosperity and an abundance of joy in all areas of your life. As you read this book, may your smile and spirit never diminish despite what you are going through.

Day 1 ~ Discover Your Authenticity

We all have something special and unique about us. What is yours? What are you known for? What do you want to be known for? Do you know that I struggled with these questions for about two years? In fact, I surveyed my closest family and friends, questioned God, reasoned with myself and even asked Google before arriving at an answer. At one point, I felt like I would discover the truth if I could get away to a quiet place to unearth my potential. The answer that it was within me was too vain, plain, cliché and simple for me to grasp fully. So today, ask yourself: "What do I have?" in other words, "Is there a skill I have not maximized?"

If you have not tapped into that skillfully, start considering what you can do with that skill or talent from this moment on. If you have, then how can you have greater influence on yourself? How can you impact others? There is always room for improvement and growth. So, close your eyes and reflect on these concepts for about five minutes. You will get the revelation. I guarantee you will. Whisper this prayer:

"I am thankful for today and the joy of living. Nothing works against me today. The works of my mind, body and soul shall prosper today. Great things are in store for my life. Today, I will rejoice and be happy because my joy is unstoppable, contagious and attractive. Today will bring me favour with God and man. I am going to be known _____ (Specify). Amen."

Declare these now with vigor, conviction and meaning:

◆ *I now commit to work my butt off to be a person of influence, power and create impact in my field.*

◆ *Negative things happen to negative people and positive things happen to positive people. I am 100% positive that I am not negative. Therefore, only that which is positive will happen in my life.*

◆ *I know that nothing happens if I don't commit to making it happen. So today, I vomit laziness, procrastination, idleness, gossiping, excuses and low expectations. I swallow wisdom, understanding, knowledge and a healthy mind. Today, I shall learn something new and exciting about my field, talent, skill or passion.*

I now affix my thumbprint / signature to seal and establish this declaration.

Day 2 ~ Power of Responsibility

Responsibility lies in the knowledge of what your commitments are and then accepting the challenge to remain in control and achieve your goals regardless. We have a good sense of responsibility to serve others most of the time. However, when it comes to us, there is often a power struggle. Responsibility is not a choice. It is a definitive action. It is not a reaction; it is an obligation. Responsible individuals make wise choices because they understand that success is a result of being proactive. To change a situation, you must act now. That is the power of   responsibility. Taking action is doing something that challenges you in every way, not because you understand what you are doing, but because you understand that your miracle depends on doing what you have to do to get where you want to be. What is it that you are afraid of doing that would advance your progress? Negate those feelings, attitudes or behaviours that inculcate irresponsibility. Renew your mind by repeating these powerful declarations now and watch how you will regain your power:

◆ *I have a renewed sense of who I am, and I refuse to have inappropriate expectations in life. I am fully alert and aware of my obligations to _____. (List them).*

◆ *I can use my power to make responsible choices for the improvement of myself, my family and the world.*

◆ *I will focus on what I need to accomplish and forget about that which distracts me from achieving my goals.*

I now affix my thumbprint / signature to seal and establish this declaration.

Day 3 ~ Shift Your Focus!

There are some days when we get things all right and then there are other days when we literally struggle with success and our daily obligations. What do I mean by this? As a single mother, I literally struggle through some days, which usually start early and end late. Throughout the day, I often juggle many roles including those of a mother, teacher, preacher, minister, sister, daughter, friend, prayer warrior and motivator. Sometimes, the roleplaying pulls me into an emotional and psychological rollercoaster. However, I have realized that coping mechanisms such as being present in the moment, remaining hopeful and releasing WHATEVER it is that kidnaps your joy, will aid significantly in your desire to move from crises to breakthroughs. Whether today is one of the days when you get it all together or one where everything is falling apart, just smile and say whatever! There is great power in shifting your focus.

Free yourself with the whatever affirmations below:

◆ *Whatever comes my way today, I am an overcomer! No problem is problematic or forever. No challenge is unsolvable. No obstacle is beyond opportunity.*

◆ *I will certainly triumph in the face of adversity and propel from crisis to calmness. (Take three deep breaths.)*

◆ *When I feel overwhelmed, I will take a deep breath and whisper, "Whatever" to destroy that feeling unconsciously and challenge myself to move past this feeling.*

I now affix my thumbprint / signature to seal and establish this declaration.

10

Day 4 ~ REACH

Why is changing habits so challenging? Why am I getting in my way of progressing? I know I need to change, but why is it so difficult? My old ways keep resurfacing! Have you ever thought about doing something, but realised that you did exactly what you planned not to do? It happens to the best of us. Today, I am imploring you to REACH.

What is R-E-A-C-H?
  R-Rely on God
  E-Expect and Execute the best.
  A-Anticipate the worst
  C- Challenge yourself to do something more or to give something more.
  H- Head for the finish line

REACH is a philosophical approach that I conceptualized while I was preparing to preach a message at church. This systematic approach employs the tools of endurance coupled with strict discipline. In order to remain level-headed and detached in the face of a setback or tough situation, you should REACH. Without a doubt, I believe that REACH is an unwritten rule of life necessary for major success in any area of life. Strict discipline keeps us committed while endurance keeps us in line and allows us to finish strong and finish well.

Ask yourself:
⇨ What am I doing that will keep me from winning or changing?
⇨ What do I have to do or change in order to win?

Now place your hand on your head, repeat these powerful affirmations and watch your life transform. I am not asking you; I am telling you. You will see positive changes henceforth.

◆ *I know where I am at fault and today this .... day of ....* *(month and year) I...................................., (full name) realise that I* *need divine help and inner strength to change.*

◆ *I will REACH to win. I will REACH in order to change. I will REACH* *for abundance.*

◆ *No one is standing in my way. I am standing in my own way and today I remove myself by_____. (Highlight or circle the steps below that apply or list the steps that you are going to take.)*

➤ discontinuing the habits of overspending, procrastinating and overeating.

➤ saving more and buying only what is needed to survive.

➤ exercising, eating healthy and / in smaller portions (portion control).

➤ starting a lucrative business I may have been delaying.

➤ planning better.

➤ not overthinking and worrying.

➤ not comparing myself with others.

➤ not trying to be a perfectionist or a control freak.

➤ not caring too much about what other people think.

➤ believing that I am good enough.

I now affix my thumbprint / signature to seal and establish this declaration.

Day 5 ~ I Will Not Be Disqualified

I agree with the apostle Paul who figured out that we are all in a race called life. Therefore, Paul urged us to run in such a way that we will win the prize. He contended that, "all run, but only one wins." Are you winning? Well, if you aren't winning, only you have the power to change that. Maybe you have one of the deadly disqualifiers (5D's) listed below, in your camp.

Deadly Disqualifiers:
➤ **Doubt**: fear, self-sabotage, low self-esteem, lack of self-confidence, lack of faith, lack of belief in your abilities.
➤ **Dead weight**: failures, baggage, hurt and pain from relationships and broken marriages/divorce, job-related issues, insecurities, dysfunctional family, inner child issues {that is, neglect, trauma or other emotional pain experienced during childhood}.
➤ **Distractions**: procrastination, lack of focus and concentration, use/misuse of technology and social media, saying yes to everything, poor organizational skills.
➤ **Discouragement**: loss of confidence, pointless focus on people or situations, demotivation, disappointment, hopelessness, lethargy, self- doubt and pity.
➤ **Defiance**: deliberate ignorance of the rules/ laws that govern the principles of success.

Finally, I have two questions to ask you. Who are your critics? Are you your biggest critic? Maybe you are too hard on yourself. First step forward is to get rid of the deadly disqualifiers. It is not that hard. Breathe in. Let go of those limitations mentally, emotionally and psychologically. Open your eyes and watch them leave. Release those deadly disqualifiers. As long as you are hell-bent that these disqualifiers are not a part of who you are, they have to leave you now. We all know the power of a made-up mind. It is powerful, just like these declarations you are going to say aloud now, to solidify and seal the deal.

Declarations for today:

◆ *I eradicate those difficult deadly disqualifiers out of my conscious and subconscious mind now.*

◆ *I refuse to be held hostage by doubt, dead weight, distractions, discouragement, defiance and their siblings.*

◆ *I call upon the I Am that is within me, who is by far greater than any other thing in and around me, to help me to win this race and to not be disqualified.*

I now affix my thumbprint / signature to seal and establish this declaration.

Day 6 ~ Purge

A purge is usually regarded as the ridding of an unwanted quality, condition or feeling. When was the last time you had a purge? Not just physically, but mentally, emotionally, financially, spiritually and psychologically. I recommend that you stop and take a few seconds or maybe minutes or days to conduct a holistic purge. Go right ahead and rid yourself of past hurt. Rid yourself of abuse from your childhood. Rid yourself of disappointment. Rid yourself of failure, unforgiveness and overspending. Rid yourself of all baggage that you are carrying into your daily activities that cripple and sabotage your ability to move forward. Live your best life and just be you. Go ahead, and then come back and repeat these powerful declarations over your life. If this activity takes a week, just do it! You will be better if you do.

Declarations:

◆ *I have purged myself holistically and I feel*_____
(Write 10 words to describe how you feel.)

◆ *I commit to conduct a holistic purge*_____
(daily, weekly, monthly, yearly).

◆ *I will avoid unnecessary harm to my body, mind, heart, soul and spirit.*

I now affix my thumbprint / signature to seal and establish this declaration.

Day 7 ~ High Achievers Don't Settle

Do I want too much out of life? Is it normal to want more out of life? Yes, yes and yes! I recently did a Google search on these questions after being told by someone close to me that I wanted too much out of life. Have you ever felt like this? Have you been told that you want too much out of life? Some people are comfortable with just getting by and that is okay. You and I are not those persons, and that is alright too. Like you, I am provoked with the "just getting by mentality," that pervades our society. The thought of settling equates suffocation to me and yes, I am grateful for all life affords me, but I also want to leave a positive mark, live well and achieve the greatest success possible.

Ordinary people create ordinary impact, but extraordinary people create extra ordinary impact. Besides, success for me is never fatally final. There are always greater depths and higher heights to be achieved. I cannot settle in life because there is another level waiting to be discovered. I guess I am an adventurer. I believe in constantly growing and pursuing something.

So, I will not be stopped because there is just something inside me so determined to be better each time. These are some of the reasons I attend research conferences and empowerment seminars, even when I don't have the last dime. I always try to find a way, so I often rely on cheap flights, motels and crazy faith. Again, I am telling you that there is absolutely nothing wrong with wanting more out of life. It is called ambition, personal development, and creating an impact. None of which is common or cheap.

Are you willing to pay the price? Whisper this prayer:

Dear God, I am extremely thankful for this moment and the endless possibilities it presents. Today, I desire to be better and this desire is instinctive and unstoppable. I will not be stopped or hindered in life. God, only you can stop me and I know You will not limit my growth because You want me to prosper and be in good health and I receive it now, by faith. Amen.

If you desire more out of life, please lift your right hand and say these powerful declarations:

◆ *I refuse to settle in life. I choose to go and grow in all areas of life.*

◆ *Nothing moves unless I move. Nothing happens unless I make it happen. Nothing changes until I change. I become only by becoming and I prosper only by prospering.*

◆ *I am uncomfortable with just getting by in life because I am a top achiever. I will not settle now or later because greater is He that is in me than He that is in the world.*

I now affix my thumbprint / signature to seal and establish this declaration.

Day 8 ~ Vision, Mission & Decision

My vision is to empower lives and enhance kingdom building. What is your vision and mission? Are you on auto pilot or are you making conscious decisions towards your goals? We are all caught in a web of pursuing nothing, unless we focus on what it is we want and how we can achieve it. Where do you want to end up? Your mission is your purpose or strategy while your vision provides the route towards accomplishing your mission. Simply put, your mission is the "what and why" whereas the vision is the "how." Start with the culmination in mind; then plot simple realistic steps towards that goal. You can never regret trying and it is never about failure.

Someone said, "Success is failure inside out." My Jamaican father often says, "the Chinese say that opportunity comes in a crisis." Consequently, the Chinese love crisis. Failure teaches wisdom and gives insights that you would not have received otherwise. It is all a matter of perspective. So, you may be faced with a crisis now, but there are ways of turning that situation into an opportunity.

I now invite you to close your eyes, dream big and focus on success for about five minutes. Now, project five to ten years in the future in a few sentences below.

My mission is to _____

and my vision is to _____

Affirmations for today:

◆ *I know my mission and have a vision for where I am heading.*

◆ *My mission is unique, and my vision is unobstructed.*

◆ *I will not act outside of my vision and mission. I will keep the focus and push myself to realise my mission because my vision is my decision and vehicle to success.*

I now affix my thumbprint / signature to seal and establish this declaration.

Day 9 ~ Deactivate Autopilot

From my early childhood days, I have always been one who goes against the norms or mundane ways of doing things. As an adult, that trait has not changed. It is good because I have my unique identity and I do not conform to restrictive, oppressive or predictable ways of existing. The moment I feel stuck or oppressed, I reflect and escape. Today I suggest that you reflect on whatever feels oppressive or mundane in your life. Then plot an escape route to whatever it is that robs you of your freedom and happiness, and just breathe. I suggest that you deactivate autopilot. Live your life with purpose and focus. You will be labelled selfish and self-centered, but guess what, I have been there. That will be a sacrifice you must be willing to make, to get back the power you have lost. It is called taking control of your life. It will be worthwhile at the end of the sorrows.

Affirmations for deactivating an autopilot lifestyle:

◆ *I refuse to lose control over my life anymore. I seize this moment and willfully withdraw my power from the hands of the oppressor(s)* _____ (List the things that held you captive.)

◆ *I choose to live a life that is centred on my God-given goals, dreams and purpose.*

◆ *I deactivate autopilot mode and activate my energy for that which I*_____(Your name) *was always destined for.*

I now affix my thumbprint / signature to seal and establish this declaration.

Day 10 ~ Knowledge Versus Application

There are knowledgeable individuals and then there are those who apply knowledge. To have knowledge is to possess information about something and to apply that knowledge is to make use of that information optimally. We should not underestimate the distinction between the two. There is a huge difference between individuals who have "head" knowledge and no application and those who have the "head" knowledge and are being practical with it. To be knowledgeable is certainly not a bad idea. We should all pursue knowledge. However, it is far more rewarding and impactful to couple knowledge with application. What is knowledge without application? What are bees without honey, trees without lumber, cows without milk?

There is a verse in the Bible that admonishes us to get understanding. It states that "wisdom is the principal thing; therefore, get wisdom and in all thy getting, get understanding!" (Proverbs 4:7) Anyway, I would rather know one thing and be renowned for my practice, than to know everything, and known for nothing. Do you prefer the same? Sometimes, Apostle Dr. Patience Oti, the founder of the Tribe, cites Proverbs 22: 29 from the King James Version which states: "Seest thou a man diligent in his business? He shall stand before kings; he shall not stand before mean men." Think about that for a moment.

Doesn't diligence mean careful and persistent work, or an activity done with painstaking effort? This diligence in business is profound. It is a call to remain focused. It is an activity. It is a practice. It is applying knowledge. The verse does not refer to a man who simply knows business; it states that a man who is constantly doing or applying knowledge will be admitted into the presence of princes and noble men. Be in the business of your calling; be it what it will. Be constant with it. Be ready and move expeditiously at it. Your reward will be to stand before kings. You shall not continue in the company of ignoble beings. Don't you agree? Let us take the knowledge out of our heads and seek to make ourselves, our families, our churches, our work environments and our countries, better places by our practices.

Let us affirm:

◆ *I will become determined in my pursuit of knowledge and I will apply knowledge.*

◆ *I will be diligent in my business.*

◆ *I will set my face as a "flint" and will NOT be disappointed.*

I now affix my thumbprint / signature to seal and establish this declaration.

Day 11 ~ Seize the Moment

You may have heard this phrase before because of its popularity, power and possibilities. However, have you seized your moment? What are you waiting on? Everyone has a defining moment. A moment that can catapult you into your great destiny. Stop gambling, complaining, procrastinating, explaining, waiting, or playing. Start praying, reading, meditating, doing, and activating. You will be successful if you go at it. May God help you so that you do not miss your defining moment.

Declarations for seizing the moment:

◆ *My defining moment shall not be missed.*

◆ *I seize every moment from here on.*

◆ *Whenever I pass through my defining moment, I will praise my God for His favour.*

I now affix my thumbprint / signature to seal and establish this declaration.

Day 12 ~ There is Greatness in the Making

By now you have a vision of where God is taking you? Does it seem impossible? Forever? Well although your vision looks good, things might not be going well for you at this very moment. I say to you however, that whatever seems bad to you now, is working for your good. I recall one year when I was victimised at my job for no apparent reason. I was ostracised and maliciously targeted by administration and a few colleagues that I trusted. It began after I resumed my maternity leave. I was told that same day that I no longer worked at the institution. My employment was terminated, and I was expected to leave my job instantly. However, I knew better, so I endured the lies, hypocrisy insults, pain, frustration and non-assignment for almost one academic year. Of course, it was a lonely road but at the end of it, I voluntarily relocated to another job, got promoted in less than a year, completed my masters in education and received one million dollars as a result of underpayment at the previous job.

Believe me when I say that there is no shortcut to success. At times, you may have to risk it all to gain more. You will suffer persecution before you arrive at the palace. Anything that looks great now, had to undergo great pressure.

Most people who are successful will tell you how challenging their journey was, but they never gave up or threw in the towel. That can be your story too. Stop taking shortcuts and setting up yourself for failure, heartbreak or death.

Don't be a Jonah or a little Red Riding Hood. Stick to the main road and arrive at your destination safely. Nothing great comes without great effort. Rome was not built in a day. Stick to your process. It will end well and at the right time.

Declarations for today:

◆ *I will remain on my path and pray. I will not take a shortcut because I am experiencing traffic on the highway. This too must pass.*

◆ *I won't get agitated by my process because greatness takes time.*

◆ *I am progressing and that will not take one day so I receive grace for endurance to finish well.*

I now affix my thumbprint / signature to seal and establish this declaration.

Day 13 ~ Every Disappointment is an Appointment

GOD,
grant me the
Serenity
to accept the things
I cannot CHANGE;
Courage
to CHANGE
the things I can;
and
Wisdom

Sometimes things just go awry, like my marriage a few years ago. For you, it might be something else and sometimes you do not know what went wrong. You were prepared, but something went wrong, and you had no control over it. Welcome to life! It is full of those moments, but I have found the antidote. The song below is forever etched in my mind:

"I don't worry when things go wrong

Jesus fills my heart with a son

It's amazing what praising can do HALLELUJAH!"

Every disappointment is truly an appointment! I have learnt to accept that which I cannot change.

Have you at least tried? I sacrificed so much to make my marriage work and it did not. Still, I have learnt so much from those disappointing moments. They have shaped my identity and impacted my life positively. As a result, I believe that those moments were divinely planned because I know the Master of the Universe is watching over the sparrow, so He is watching over me.

Therefore, no crisis can affect me without His approval and deliverance. Hence, disappointing moments are designed to add to the fabric of life. So, embrace the lesson you learnt. It was beneficial! Also, never discount that lesson. What did you learn from that experience? In other words, what was the teachable moment? It had to be worth something. If you had not experienced this "unforeseen" challenge, you could not have learned that valuable lesson. You should applaud yourself. Undoubtedly, process over product is my emphasis here.

You must persevere to the end to understand! Again, every disappointment is an opportunity to grow!

Declarations for your day:

◆ *Lord help me to see, understand, appreciate and value the opportunity that is present in my crisis.*

◆ *Whatever comes my way in the days ahead will not tear me apart but will build me up!*

◆ *I am in this race of life for the process and not for the product, for it is the process that gives me wisdom, knowledge and understanding.*

I now affix my thumbprint / signature to seal and establish this declaration.

Day 14 ~ Keys to Generational Wealth

My eldest son Mikhail has the task of selecting our nightly scripture before we retire to bed. During the COVID19 pandemic he selected a hidden gem which I will share with you. It contains a secret to wealth. Please read with understanding.

Ecclesiastes 11: 1- 6
Invest in Many Ventures

1. *Ship your grain across the sea;*
after many days you may receive a return.
2. *Invest in seven ventures, yes, in eight;*
you do not know what disaster may come upon the land.
3. *If clouds are full of water, they pour rain on the earth.*
Whether a tree falls to the south or to the north, in the place where it falls, there it will lie.
4. *Whoever watches the wind will not plant;*
whoever looks at the clouds will not reap.
5. *As you do not know the path of the wind,*
or how the body is formed[a] in a mother's womb,
so you cannot understand the work of God,
the Maker of all things.
6. *Sow your seed in the morning,*
and at evening let your hands not be idle,
for you do not know which will succeed,
whether this or that,
or whether both will do equally well.

I encourage you to meditate upon and work Ecclesiastes 11: 1- 6 until financial fitness is achieved. This is one revelation I got from the verses.

3 M' s for Financial Fitness:

Use your gift: **Magnify it! Market it! Monetize it!**

You can only win with that strategy. You are guaranteed financial finesse using these principles from the golden book.

Affirmations:

◆ *I am not lazy, so I will attain generational wealth.*

◆ *I am wealthy and healthy.*

◆ *I am prosperous and glorious.*

I now affix my thumbprint / signature to seal and establish this declaration.

Day 15 ~ Do It!

Stop the talking; it is action time! I preached one Sunday during the novel COVID19 pandemic about using what you have. I used the story in the Bible where Jesus fed a multitude with five loaves and two small fish. Jesus raised one question that stood out then and is still relevant today. He asked, "What do you have?" I have been pondering this question ever since that message. I have challenged myself to use whatever I have to advance my well-being and that of others. Today I posit this simple, but life-changing question to you: What do you have? Use it, or something or someone will use you. Meditate on what you have that you can monetize - skills, assets, gifting; anything can be valuable if you use it!

Affirmations:

◆ *I have_____(list them). Show me now God how I can monetize it/ them. (Record in your book how you can use each item you listed here.)*

◆ *I will do as I have written, and it shall end well. I will seek knowledge and understanding to execute this vision.*

◆ *People with knowledge and understanding in this regard, will locate and help me as I seek to apply the knowledge that I have gained.*

I now affix my thumbprint / signature to seal and establish this declaration.

Day 16 ~ Size Matters

What Works for Me? This is an important question, but seldom pondered, because one size does not fit all. You must find what works for you. What is your situation and how can you fix it? No one knows what is best for you, but you! You are your best solution. Not that others cannot guide you. Certainly, they can, but at the end of the day, you hold the answers to your biggest problems. Others can recommend and suggest, but if it does not help to alleviate the situation in your best interest, then it isn't your size. I pray that God grants you the wisdom of Solomon, the knowledge of Queen Esther and the understanding of Job, to discern your toughest situations.

Declarations for the day:

◆ *I will exercise my faith to know what my fate is.*

◆ *Wisdom, knowledge and understanding are my portion.*

◆ *All things are working for my good because God said so.*

I now affix my thumbprint / signature to seal and establish this declaration.

Day 17 ~ Breaking the News

Have you delayed telling someone something for a while now? I know from my experience that breaking some news can be exceedingly difficult or even painful to do. However, because it must be done, you will need to use tact and honesty to ensure that you navigate the situation well. Let me repeat, tact and honesty are two qualities that you will need when you are breaking any news to anyone. Likewise, prayer and meditation help to keep you calm and focused. When you are calm, you can make better decisions regarding how to approach any situation. Just use love as your benchmark.

Declare these with a loud voice:

◆ *I will be a carrier of only good news. I will have great reports and testimonies.*

◆ *If I must bear and carry bad news it shall be well-sent and well-received.*

◆ *I choose to remain calm even in conflicting and confusing times.*

I now affix my thumbprint / signature to seal and establish this declaration.

Day 18 ~ I Won't Miss my Divine Helpers

Many of us either love to be helped or do not accept help easily. Neither of the behaviours is beneficial. Sometimes we might be praying for a particular matter and when God answers, we either do not recognize it or receive it. I pray for you today that you will not miss your divine helpers. You will be fully alert and prepared to receive what you have been praying for. You will not miss your helpers, neither will your children nor their children. Not now, not ever!

Declarations:

◆ *I am a candidate for miracles, signs and wonders.*

◆ *I am at the right places, at the right times, with the right people, for the right things to happen to, and for me.*

◆ *Helpers of my destiny, divine connectors, people of influence, arise, locate me and perform your duty now!*

I now affix my thumbprint / signature to seal and establish this declaration.

Day 19 ~ Prayer Still Works

There is nothing that prayer cannot change. You have a challenge; I dare you to pray about it. That is where your answers lie. People who pray about everything, conquer anything. What is it that you need help with? Is there a burden that you are carrying into your daily activities?

Let us pray about it. Ask a good friend to help you take it to God in prayer. The prayer of agreement will alleviate that stubborn problem and victory will be inevitable.

Let us pray:

Creator of the universe, I humbly come before Your throne of grace and mercy. Forgive me for past and present sins. I ask for Your intervention in this situation _____
(name it). I claim divine help supernaturally. I cannot find solace unless You come to my rescue. Because I cannot move forward, I cast my cares upon You for You care for me. I thank You for Your help and favour. You are truly awesome and divine. In Jesus' name I pray, with thanksgiving. Amen. (Feel free to continue praying.)

Declarations:

◆ *I will pray about everything because prayer is my answer.*

◆ *God, teach me to pray and cease not. Give me a healthy appetite for prayer. Let prayer be my first thought and not an afterthought.*

◆ *God, make me a prayer warrior. Teach me to pray. Thank you for answering my prayer.*

I now affix my thumbprint / signature to seal and establish this declaration.

Day 20 ~ Expect the Unimaginable

Expectation breathes manifestations. Accordingly, if you expect nothing, you receive nothing. I understand that you may not want to expect too much in order to avoid disappointment and regrets. While I agree with you to some extent, the opposite is equally true. If you don't expect much, you set up yourself for disappointment and regrets anyway. I usually don't reveal all of what I expect, especially from relationships. You should leave room for what is to be. Time is the master of it all. Time reveals the true character in you as well as
in others.

Yes, time and situations usually reveal character, but still lift your expectancy. Check your expectations as they give rise to hope and hope gives way to actualization.

Declarations for today:

◆ *They that put their trust in the Lord shall never be disappointed, so I shake off low expectancy. I dismiss what people told me I could not accomplish.*

◆ *I have high expectations and I will no longer lower the bar of hopefulness out of fear of disappointment, hurt, failure and regret.*

◆ *Today is the opportune day for me to see the manifestations of my "expected end." (Jerimiah 29:11)*

I now affix my thumbprint / signature to seal and establish this declaration.

Day 21 ~ Do What You Were Called to Do!

Leaders should raise their subordinates to be even greater than them. Some leaders are a rebel against God's work in your life! Sadly, I have encountered a few of those types of leaders, even amongst the religious community. The leaders who do not want you to utilise your gift/s outside their territory are dream killers. They do not want you to "outshine" them. That is jealousy. That is not a place where you should be. Besides, any environment that is putting a limit on your potential, is not one in which you will thrive. Everyone is a work in progress as you are. Nobody is perfect and they are not God, so you should not be too depressed about their refusal to support you.

If you allow anyone to stifle your growth, you are giving that person control over your destiny. Do not allow anyone to kill your dreams. It does not matter if it is your pastor, partner, professor or parent. No one should be allowed to stifle your dreams. If you need a jump start to do all that you have been placed on this universe to accomplish, please forgive yourself for confining your gifts to a box, then repeat these declarations:

◆ *I forgive myself for feeling like I cannot utilize my gifts.*

◆ *God is with me, so I cannot be disgraced or humiliated by household enemies.*

◆ *I am a brand. I will keep up my brand. I will not be stopped by man with limited perspectives.*

I now affix my thumbprint / signature to seal and establish this declaration.

Day 22 ~ Don't Let Jealousy Undermine You

Being a spiritual person is not being stupid, but at times you must stoop in order to conquer. Jealousy results in a lot of inhumane things. Smile, when you see a person for who they really are. Peculiar situations reveal motives and heart postures. First, look at the small things that happen to you and watch the behaviour of those closest to you. Next, look at motives. Learn to read a person's intention. Use emotional intelligence to do this. Then look at actions.

Sometimes you might have to do cross checks to validate your assertions. Also, for reliability and credibility purposes, it is advised that you triangulate your data. Finally, look at the heart posture. What is in a person's heart, flows to his/her speech, attitude and behaviour. Remember that by their fruit, you will know them.

Declarations:

◆ *If there is any form of jealousy within me, I vomit it now and I release those whom I have been jealous of.*

◆ *I will not be jealous of others as I don't want others to be jealous of me. I forgive those who are jealous of me.*

◆ *Let those who are jealous of me be blessed and favoured, so that they will have no need to be jealous of me or others.*

I now affix my thumbprint / signature to seal and establish this declaration.

Day 23 ~ Loyalty Over Control

There is a thin line between loyalty and control. Loyalty is multi-directional, in that, the quality flows from one individual to another. Control on the other hand is one directional and aims at manipulating others. What exactly do I mean? Many friends, pastors, employers and even family members tend to control those around them because of egotistical and narcissistic behaviours. Even worse, many are not aware that they are being manipulated and others upon realization, are ridiculed and then labelled wrongfully as being "selfish" or "disloyal." I say they are only tired of being controlled. What do you say?

Declarations:

◆ *I am deliberately rebelling against any form of control and manipulation that masquerades as loyalty.*

◆ *Only God controls my mind, body and soul.*

◆ *I am loyal and I reject control and manipulation (Repeat 3 times).*

I now affix my thumbprint / signature to seal and establish this declaration.

Day 24 ~ Remove the Full Stop

Are you in a season where you think that you have reached your peak? Please, don't put a full stop where a comma is supposed to be. If you do, you may have changed the meaning of the subject. Many people err by putting an end where they should be starting or continuing. I have done so many times in the past. However, I have learnt so much from those seasons. Let me remind you that only time will tell, so hang in there. My aunt often reminds me that it will be long, but not forever. This statement is true.

Here are three powerful declarations to help you remove the full stop wherever you have mistakenly placed a comma:

◆ *Today, I remove my emotions from my situation and reflect on what I am destined to achieve.*

◆ *I may be facing a red sea or a full stop moment, but I will not stop here permanently. This moment is therefore temporary.*

◆ *What the Creator has placed within me cannot be halted. This crisis shall pass, and I will overcome it victoriously.*

I now affix my thumbprint / signature to seal and establish this declaration.

Day 25 ~ Get Ready to be Exposed

The closer you get to God the more exposure you will face. God will reveal to you your character defects for you to submit to Him for workmanship. You were not born with those ungodly traits. As you journey through life, crises happen. However, choose to change those ways. Do not remain the same. The choice is yours to take but I can tell you from experience that it is not an easy pill to swallow when God opens your eyes to your flaws. It is not easy to see them up close, but it is necessary in order to elevate to the next level of your spiritual career.

The work that God is doing on your character is a prerequisite for something greater in your life. Where God is taking you is significant. All the great men and women in the Bible had character flaws. You cannot forget that David had a lustful eye and murdered his boss; Moses had anger and Paul was a persecutor. Those character flaws did not stop them from achieving their God-given assignments and purposes, so neither will yours.

Repeat these affirmations:

◆ *I am exposed and empowered.*

◆ *I am exalted by God.*

◆ *I am using my character flaws for kingdom assignment.*

I now affix my thumbprint / signature to seal and establish this declaration.

Day 26 ~ Eviction Notice

An eviction notice is a letter sent by a landlord to a tenant describing a violation or termination of the rental agreement. This is known as an eviction notice or a "notice to quit." Upon receipt of the notice, the tenant will have a specified number of days to either comply or vacate the property. Today is the day you will serve an eviction notice to whatever challenges you face. In other words, tell that situation to go, be it a terminal illness, poverty, marital problems, barrenness and or unfruitfulness, fear or whatever it is.

You know exactly what your biggest challenge is. I suggest that you serve it an eviction notice right now. I do not know anyone who has ever gotten through a challenge by keeping it. Arise and tell that stubborn, intergenerational curse to leave your body, mind, soul, environment and family right now. Tell that challenge or challenges to find another place of residence because you have suffered too long and will no longer tolerate the inconvenience being caused. That challenge has violated every promise God made to you and your generation. If you check your Bible you will understand exactly where I am coming from.

Carefully examine these three declarations which are loaded with passages from the bible and declare them aloud with me now:

◆ *Today I serve eviction notice to:* _____
(name every challenge in your life.) *I*_____
(insert your name) *terminate every evil contract signed knowingly or unknowingly with your kingdom and terminate every evil rental agreement in my family that has been working contrary to the word of God in my life and in the life of my family.*

◆ *I command every challenge:* (name every challenge with holy anger) *to find another place of residence. You have been served notice to quit with immediate effect because who the Son sets free is free indeed!*
42

◆ *I boldly declare that I am the head and not the tail; therefore, the works of my hands prosper.*

Continue to boldly repeat these declarations daily and watch God's power of deliverance melt that challenge away for you to testify of His resurrection power in the land of the living.

I now affix my thumbprint / signature to seal and establish this declaration.

Day 27 ~ Those Little Rats

One Saturday night, when I arrived home after visiting my parents, I saw a little creature in my kitchen. It was a mouse. So, the next morning, I decided to purchase some rat baits. To my surprise, the following morning, I found not one, nor two, but three of those creatures lying helplessly on the glue trap. I was pleasantly surprised. Then I thought to myself, what about those things in my life that I utterly despise, those negative habits and behaviours that I don't usually think of ways of getting rid of them? Maybe in the same way I trapped and rid my house of the mice, I could quite easily find a way to trap and get rid of my negative ways or situations.

As I pondered, I realized that was as easy as 123. I don't know what it is that you have in your life that you do not like or want to do away with. It may be a bad habit or behaviour. You can do something about it today. It's as easy as 123:

1. *Identify it.*

2. *Think about the best solution to achieve the desired results.*

3. *Simply do it.*

It is all in the action. Your change comes in doing. Yet, few people are doing things to change their lives positively. Do not let your fears freak you out; kill them instead. You can paralyze them. Absolutely no situation is beyond your ability to control. If you cannot control a situation, you can control how you react to it. No habit is beyond your ability to change. You can let them go.

Today I want you to repeat these powerful declarations with me. As you repeat them, believe in your heart that whatever it is that you want to get rid of, will go immediately.

Declarations:

◆ *I refuse to be controlled by any circumstance, thought, virus, habit or behaviour that is negatively affecting me or my loved ones.*

◆ *I consciously break every stronghold over me that is limiting my ability to prosper and be in good health.*

◆ *Today I choose to let go of whatever is holding me back mentally, physically, emotionally, psychologically and spiritually. I inhale a fresh air of stability, love, peace, joy and favour.*

I now affix my thumbprint / signature to seal and establish this declaration.

Day 28 ~ Narratives of the Oppressed

Never forget that reading and writing are essential ingredients to becoming extraordinary. The bible admonishes that people suffer because of "lack of knowledge". Equally important is that of speaking our truth to power because our words are fundamental in creating the future we desire. Marcus Garvey puts it this way:

> *The pen is mightier than the sword, but the tongue is mightier than them both put together. There shall be no solution to this race problem until you, yourselves, strike the blow for liberty. What you do today that is worthwhile, inspires others to act at some future time. Intelligence rules the world, ignorance carries the burden. Therefore, remove yourself as far as possible from ignorance and seek as far as possible to be intelligent.*

For too long we have underestimated the power of our narratives in important matters concerning race, justice, government, education, equity and other critical aspects of life. We have suffered injustice at the hands of prejudiced, oppressive systems and structures. Look at those amongst us, who use their skin colour, wealth or power to act superior and privileged.

The hegemonic discourse that the ruling class tells in order to justify their power and maintain wealth, can be challenged by us through our narratives. Always remember that our voices are critical in shaping our worldview. Simply put, our narrative allows for freedom from oppression because our expression eliminates ignorance and facilitates knowledge production. Therefore, I urge you to put your thoughts to paper, kindle, audio or whatever method possible and express, explore, share, listen, empower, encourage, and reflect on our experiences. Haven't you heard that if you want to hide something from a black person, put it into a book? The narratives of the oppressed will not only challenge that claim but debunk it forever.

People of colour, I dare you to frustrate whatever is frustrating you and externalize what you are internalizing through your narratives. Pun intended; that which is black and white, counts.

Declarations for today:

◆ *I am a writer of valuable material. I speak truth to power and create the changes that I want to see in the world with my words.*

◆ *I will take advantage of every opportunity to write and thereby create narratives that will dismantle the social order.*

◆ *I will read more, speak more and write more. My narrative is an ammunition to deconstruct inequitable systems that perpetuate oppression.*

I now affix my thumbprint / signature to seal and establish this declaration.

Day 29 ~ Be Your Own Competition

There are so many people who cannot be genuinely happy for others. They refuse to lift others up or let others shine. We should understand that letting others shine and enjoying their moment of success, will not stop us from shining. Let us always remember that there is something that we have that others will need, and the reverse is also true. It is a mutual exchange and not a competition.

Healthy competition is good; however, in creating impact and walking in your purpose, unhealthy competitive behaviour is not necessary. If you are going to compete, be your only competitor and set standards to live by. A standard safeguard your beliefs, values and mores. Tony Robbins purports that, "The difference in people is their standard." Raise the standard of your life and refuse to lower your standards for persons who have low or no standards. They are ignorant, lazy, fearful, narcissistic, entitled, critical and haughty.

Let your standards act as a guide for how you operate. Be a conduit of blessings to others, so rejoice when they rejoice, and mourn with them when they mourn. When you set standards and avoid unhealthy competition, you will always win.

Today, declare these affirmations with me:

◆ *I will not act outside of the standards that I have established.*

◆ *The competition with myself is never over, so I will not get complacent or lackadaisical.*

◆ *I will not lower my standards, but I will raise them from time to time.*

I now affix my thumbprint / signature to seal and establish this declaration.

Day 30 ~ That's a "You" Problem!

How do you deal with people whose real issue is not with you, but they deflect it towards you? If everyone confirms that your behaviour or attitude is negative, then a high possibility exists that they are 99.99 percent accurate. Otherwise, remind yourself that you are not the source of their problems. Tell them, clearly, "It is a "you" problem." Some people are so unhappy that they take pleasure in making everyone around them unhappy all the time. They may be scarred from childhood or they might just have some inner work to do. Whatever the case might be, remember it is a "you" problem. What it means is that they have a problem, and they need professional help. If they are open to receiving help, that is awesome. However, if they refuse help, then ignore the behaviour, but not the person.

There are so many people who deflect their issues on innocent people consciously or unconsciously. Then, there are others who seek a friend ONLY when they need help. That is called "using" people. The point here is that you must learn to filter out such individuals. You can do this by being present physically, but unavailable emotionally. This might help you to deal with some of the difficult personalities you encounter.

Declare these with me today:

◆   *I am wholesome and complete the way I am*

_____

(say the name/s of the individual or organization) *has a problem and it is not me!*

◆ *I will not let the behaviour of*_____ (say their name/s again) *allow me to be emotionally drained or judgmental about myself.*

I now affix my thumbprint / signature to seal and establish this declaration.

Day 31 ~ The Power of No

For many years, I battled with guilt for saying no, until I attended one of Bishop TD Jakes' conferences and learnt the art of saying no from Dr. Anita Phillips. You should try to say no too. It gives you control over your life and it is your personal right. Saying no might be disappointing to others at times, but when you say no, you are now making that commitment to yourself, to value your health and sanity. Saying no is not about being selfish. At times, we overextend ourselves and suffer the consequences of feeling burnt out or used by people who often take kindness for weakness.

Moreover, saying no helps you to stay focused on what is important. Saying no, gives you autonomy. Saying no, helps you to achieve your work and life balance. Do not try to please people at your expense. Let us say these declarations and please do not say no.

◆ *I refuse to overextend myself in order to please others.*

◆ *I will learn to say no without feeling guilty about it.*

◆ *Saying no, is my privilege.* (Repeat two more times).

I now affix my thumbprint / signature to seal and establish this declaration.

Day 32 ~ Dream Death

Are your goals and dreams dying? Be reminded that a death can be natural, accidental, suicidal, homicidal, undetermined, and pending. Death by natural causes is often recorded on death records as the cause of a person's death due to internal factors, like a medical condition or a disease. Whereas cancer is not considered a natural cause of death, death from natural causes might be a stroke, heart attack, illness, or infection. Inversely, death caused by active intervention or external factors, like trauma from an accident is known as unnatural death.

Without a doubt, many of our desires, dreams, purpose, vision, goals and destiny are painfully dying from natural and unnatural causes daily. In fact, some people live carefree lifestyles when it comes to their personal and professional development. They believe it is the responsibility of another to unlock their true potential to create an impact. Then there are some individuals who want others to be successful, but not themselves. Let that not be true for you. Just as your physical health is your responsibility, so is the realization of your dreams and the maximisation of your full potential. Listen to your inner being and dig deeply for your calling.

Break the bondage of self-sabotaging, excuses and procrastination. On the flip side, you may have lost a job, marriage, relationship, relative or your good health due to a natural or unnatural cause. Be encouraged today. Stop worrying about things that are falling apart, because if God brought you to it, He will bring you through it. So, rest assured that whatever happens, you can still achieve your desired end. The question therefore is: What is your desired end? Dream big and then hunt for it until that attraction is a lived reality.

Now repeat these three declarations with me:

◆ *Things do not happen to me, they happen for me. In order to live my best life here and now, I* _____ _____(say your name) *refuse to have my purpose die naturally, accidentally, through suicide, homicide or undeterminably.*

◆ *There is a time and season for everything under the sun. So, when it is time for me to leave this earth, I will go, having lived a full life and having achieved my God-given assignment here on earth.*

◆ *I am thankful that my dreams will not die of natural or unnatural causes, because I am a part of the bigger vision that I cannot fully see, but I know that the expected end is near and it is good. My dreams will not be pending indefinitely.*

I now affix my thumbprint / signature to seal and establish this declaration.

Day 33 ~ One For The Road

In Jamaica, we have a popular saying, "One for the road." This phrase is one which alludes hope and assurance. Also, it is much like a bonus or gratuity. As a child hopes that mommy and daddy will always be there, rest assured that our Heavenly Father is looking out for our every need, every day. You cannot read any book forever, so this book has come to an end. Your hope does not stop here. I am quite sure you know that. However, in the days that lie ahead, rest assured that your smile and spirit will not diminish, despite what you are going through. Keep calm, God can do it every time.

Therefore, I implore you, chart your own course. Dream your own dreams. Live in faith. Go for it. Whatever that IT is.

Let us repeat these powerful declarations together:

◆ *I am fearfully and wonderfully made, destined for more than I can think, ask or even imagine. I will live my best life now because hope deferred is hope denied.*

◆ *I will try again, even if it means dying. I will make a move, knowing that if I make a move, things will move in pleasant places for me.*

◆ *I live in the sunshine of hope, the rainbow of peace, and the clouds of joy. As numerous as the stars above, are those persons who are divinely assigned to help me achieve greatness.*

I now affix my thumbprint / signature to seal and establish this declaration.

www.ingramcontent.com/pod-product-compliance
Lightning Source LLC
LaVergne TN
LVHW041209080426
835508LV00008B/870